Alfi and the Dark

The illustrations are for Sally, Tony, Alfi
and Frederika, with love

British Library Cataloguing in Publication Data
Miles, Sally
Alfi and the dark.
I. Title   II. Le Cain, Errol
823'.914 [J]   PZ7

ISBN 0-340-40945-2

Text copyright © The Estate of Sally Miles 1988
Illustrations copyright © Errol le Cain 1988

First published 1988

Published by Hodder and Stoughton Children's Books,
a division of Hodder and Stoughton Ltd,
Mill Road, Dunton Green, Sevenoaks, Kent TN13 2YJ

Printed in Singapore

All rights reserved

Alfi and the Dark
by SALLY MILES

With pictures by ERROL LE CAIN

HODDER AND STOUGHTON
LONDON SYDNEY AUCKLAND TORONTO

Alfi was lying asleep in his bed
When he suddenly woke with a thought, and he said,
"If I switch on the light I'll be able to see
But where will the Dark go? Where will it be?"

The Dark, of course, could hear every word
And laughed to itself and thought, "How absurd
That nobody knows where I go when it's light.
Perhaps, if they knew, it would give them a fright!"

Alfi tossed and he turned and he tried counting sheep,
But try as he might he could not get to sleep.
He wanted the answer. He wanted to know.
So he sat up and cried, "Dark, where *do* you go?"

He sat up and waited, but no answer came.
Then to his surprise someone whispered his name.
Alfi was scared and thought, "What shall I do?"
Then in a cracked voice he asked, "Dark, is that you?"

All round the room he could hear the Dark stir.
Again Alfi waited. Had the Dark heard?
"Dark, is that you I can hear but not see?
Then a husky voice answered, "Yes, Alfi, it's ME!"

Alfi jumped up and down and he screeched with delight.
"Oh! Where do you go when I switch on the light?"
"I'll tell you," said Dark, "if you don't tell a soul.
If you do, woe betide you, for no one must know."

"But first, Alfi, say, have you any idea
Where I might go to when I disappear?"
He tried hard to think but his mind was a blank.
Not one idea came and poor Alfi's heart sank.

"Come on," said Dark, "try not to despair.
I'll give you a clue – I could be anywhere!"
Alfi thought for a moment, then jumped in the air.
"I've got it! I've got it! I'm sure I know where!"

"If I switch on the light, as I'm blinking my eyes,
You are up and away and are high in the sky.
You're passing the moon, passing Venus and Mars,
And passing the sun and passing the stars —

Till far out of sight, but still gathering pace,
Through glittering galaxies far out in space,
You reach your own planet. It's there where you go —
To the edge of the universe. See, there, I know!"

"Why don't you answer me? Why don't you speak?
Are you teasing or trying to play hide and seek?"
"Forgive me," said Dark, "for a moment my mind
Was distracted. I'm sorry. Don't think me unkind.

I'll answer you, Alfi, and you can depend
On me telling my secret if you'll be my friend."
"Of course, Dark, I'll promise to be friends with you,
And I'll tell all my friends to be friends with you, too!"

Dark was so happy he laughed with delight.
"Now I'll tell where I go when you switch on the light.
The answer is simple and you'll be amazed –
I NEVER GO ANYWHERE!" Alfi was dazed.

"What, nowhere at all? Dark, what do you mean?
Where do you go when you're not here with me?"
"But I *am* here. The problem is, when the light's on
You can't see me, Alfi, the light is too strong.

I'm here in your cupboard, but hard as you try,
When you open the door you can't see me, and why?
'Cause the light gets inside. It's the same with each drawer –
When you let in the light you can see me no more.

"The same with the universe. I'm everywhere,
But when the sun's shining you can't see I'm there.
The moon and the planets, they all know me well.
It's the same with your room. See, I promised I'd tell!"

"Oh Dark, thank you Dark, how exciting it's been.
Now I'll never be frightened to wake up and see
That you're there all around me. I'll whisper your name
And know that you'll answer and be just the same."

Alfi crawled back to bed and he snuggled right down.
Then he went fast asleep without making a sound.
"There," whispered Dark, "lies my very best friend,
Who now knows the answer!" and that is THE END!

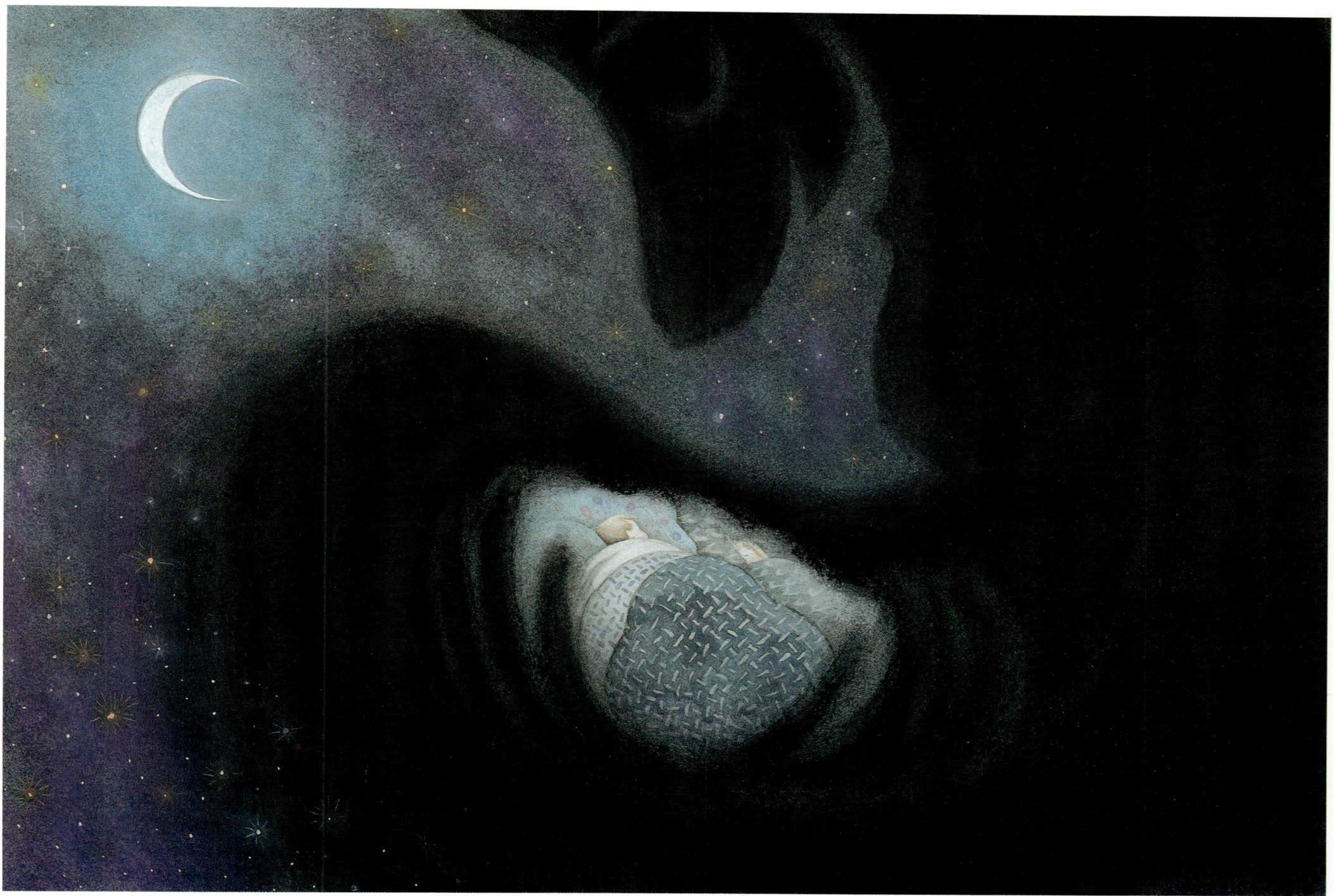